Quiet Time With God

Listening for God's Still, Small voice

Christine Spicer

Copyright © 2021 by Christine Spicer
All rights reserved. No part of this publication may be reproduced, distributed, or transmitted in any form or by any means, including photocopying, recording, or other electronic or mechanical methods, without the prior written permission of the publisher, except in the case of brief quotations embodied in critical reviews and certain other noncommercial uses permitted by copyright law.

Contents

Prayer Point:
Spouse 6

Prayer Point:
Patience 8

Prayer Point:
Anointing 10

Prayer Point:
Protection 12

Prayer Point:
Anger 14

Prayer Point:
Your Whole House Shall Be Saved 16

Prayer Point:
Anxiety 18

Prayer Point:
Depression 20

Prayer Point:
Favor 22

Prayer Point:
Power In The Blood 24

Prayer Point:
God's Image - My Image 26

Prayer Point:
Authority 28

Prayer Point:
Prejudice 30

Prayer Point:
Life 32

Prayer Point:
Armor of God 34

Prayer Point:
Hopelessness 36

Prayer Point:
Draw Close to God 38

Prayer Point:
Emotional Healing 40

Prayer Point:
Overcome Procrastination 42

Prayer Point:
Go Of The Past 44

Prayer Point:
Have Faith In God 46

Prayer Point:
Humility 48

Prayer Point:
Blessed 50

Prayer Point:
Gratitude 52

Prayer Point:
Spiritual Hunger 54

Prayer Point:
Selfish 56

Prayer Point:
Be Of Good Courage 58

Prayer Point:
Worship Him 60

Prayer Point:
Identity 62

Prayer Point:
Strengthen The Inner Man 64

Prayer Point:
God's Love 66

Prayer Point:
A Life Turned Around 68

Prayer Point:
Grace 70

Prayer Point:
Purpose 72

Prayer Point:
Insecurity 74

Prayer Point:
You Are Chosen 76

Prayer Point:
Living In The Overflow 78

Prayer Point:
You Hold The Key 80

Prayer Point:
Purify My Heart 82

Prayer Point:
Confusion 84

Prayer Point:
Overcoming Your Flaws 86

Prayer Point:
Hear The Voice Of God 88

Prayer Point:
You Already Have It 90

Prayer Point:
Determination 92

Prayer Point:
See Through Your Spiritual Eyes 94

Prayer Point:
Decree And Declare 96

Prayer Point:
More Than Conquerors 98

Prayer Point:
Deliverance 100

Prayer Point:
Binding and Loosing 102

Prayer Point:
Overcome Bad Habits, Strongholds, Addictions 104

Prayer Point:
Children 106

Prayer Point:
Eating Surrounded By Enemies 108

PRAYER POINT:

Spouse

INSPIRATIONAL QUOTE

"Love is not what you say; love is what you do."
John Hagee

1 Corinthians 13:4-8

Love is patient and kind. Love is not jealous or boastful or proud or rude. Love does not demand its own way. Love is not irritable, and it keeps no record of when it has been wronged. It is never glad about injustice but rejoices when ever the truth wins out. Love never gives up, never loses faith, is always hopeful, and endures through every circumstance. Love will last forever, but prophecy and speaking in unknown languages and special knowledge will all disappear.

Prayer

Father I thank you for my Godly spouse.
I thank you for giving them spiritual wisdom.
I ask that you open up their eyes of understanding.
I ask that you help them when they can not find
the way. Holy Spirit, lead them into righteousness
in all of their ways. Jesus, they are Your child. You love
them more than I do, so I choose to step back and
submit to You and allow You to work in their
heart. I decree and declare that you have given my
spouse a new heart and put a new spirit within them.
In Jesus' name. Amen!

Weekly Devotions

YOU KEEP HIM IN PERFECT PEACE WHOSE MIND IS STAYED ON YOU, BECAUSE HE TRUSTS IN YOU. TRUST IN THE LORD FOREVER, FOR THE LORD GOD IS AN EVERLASTING ROCK. (ISAIAH 26:3-4)

Day Date Scripture

Special Notes

Day Date Scripture

Day Date Scripture

Day Date Scripture

Prayer List

Day Date Scripture

Day Date Scripture

Day Date Scripture

PRAYER POINT:

Patience

Inspirational Quote

"No matter what's happening, choose to be happy. Don't focus on what's wrong. Find something positive in your life."-
Joel Osteen

Galatians 5:22-23

But when the Holy Spirit controls our lives, he will produce this kind of fruit in us: love, joy, peace, patience, kindness, goodness, faithfulness, gentleness, and self-control. Here there is no conflict with the law.

Prayer

In the name of Jesus, Your Spirit lives in me,
I have the fruit of the Spirit therefore I have
patience. I will not lose heart and grow weary
and faint in acting nobly and doing right.
Lord, thank You for showing me how patient
You are. I choose to be happy when the way is
rough because it gives my patience a chance to grow.
In the name of Jesus, Amen.

Weekly Devotions

YOU KEEP HIM IN PERFECT PEACE WHOSE MIND IS STAYED ON YOU, BECAUSE HE TRUSTS IN YOU. TRUST IN THE LORD FOREVER, FOR THE LORD GOD IS AN EVERLASTING ROCK. (ISAIAH 26:3-4)

Day Date Scripture

Day Date Scripture

Day Date Scripture

Day Date Scripture

Day Date Scripture

Day Date Scripture

Day Date Scripture

Special Notes

Prayer List

PRAYER POINT:

Anointing

INSPIRATIONAL QUOTES

"God will dare to do the impossible in your life if you dare to step across the faith line."
Kenneth Copeland

Isaiah 61:1

The Spirit of the Sovereign Lord is upon me, because the Lord has appointed me to bring good news to the poor. He has sent me to comfort the broken hearted and to announce that captives will be released and prisoners will be freed.

Prayer

Father, Your word says that the Spirit of the Lord God is upon me because the Lord has anointed me to bring good news. I thank you Lord, for You have anointed me with oil and gladness. Just like the disciples, I am called to drive out unclean spirits and anoint with oil on many who are sick and cure them. I am seated at the right hand of the Father and no weapon formed against me shall prosper. In Jesus' name, Amen.

Weekly Devotions

YOU KEEP HIM IN PERFECT PEACE WHOSE MIND IS STAYED ON YOU, BECAUSE HE TRUSTS IN YOU. TRUST IN THE LORD FOREVER, FOR THE LORD GOD IS AN EVERLASTING ROCK. (ISAIAH 26:3-4)

Day _____ Date _____ Scripture _____

Day _____ Date _____ Scripture _____

Day _____ Date _____ Scripture _____

Day _____ Date _____ Scripture _____

Day _____ Date _____ Scripture _____

Day _____ Date _____ Scripture _____

Day _____ Date _____ Scripture _____

Special Notes

Prayer List

PRAYER POINT:

Protection

INSPIRATIONAL QUOTES

"God loves you just as much as He loves Jesus!" - Kenneth Copeland

Psalm 91:10-11

No evil will conquer you; no plague will come near your dwelling.
For he orders his angels to protect you wherever you go.

Prayer

Father, thank You that You send Your angels concerning me, to guard me in all of my ways. Thank You for the blood of Jesus. Your word says no evil will befall me. No plague will approach my tent. I will keep my mind and thoughts focused on what Your word says.

Thank You for Your protection. In Jesus' name, Amen.

Weekly Devotions

YOU KEEP HIM IN PERFECT PEACE WHOSE MIND IS STAYED ON YOU, BECAUSE HE TRUSTS IN YOU. TRUST IN THE LORD FOREVER, FOR THE LORD GOD IS AN EVERLASTING ROCK. (ISAIAH 26:3-4)

Day Date Scripture

Special Notes

Day Date Scripture

Day Date Scripture

Day Date Scripture

Prayer List

Day Date Scripture

Day Date Scripture

Day Date Scripture

PRAYER POINT:

Anger

INSPIRATIONAL QUOTES

"The degree of your anger over correction equals the measure of your pride."
John Paul Jackson

Ecclesiastes 7:9

Do not hasten in your spirit to be angry, For anger rests in the bosom of fools.

Prayer

Father, I thank you for self-control. I am slow to anger and have great understanding; I am not like he who is hasty of spirit. I follow the example of the Lord, who is merciful and gracious, slow to anger and plenteous in mercy and loving-kindness. I choose to forgive, I will not hold any anger towards anybody. In Jesus' name, Amen.

Weekly Devotions

YOU KEEP HIM IN PERFECT PEACE WHOSE MIND IS STAYED ON YOU, BECAUSE HE TRUSTS IN YOU. TRUST IN THE LORD FOREVER, FOR THE LORD GOD IS AN EVERLASTING ROCK. (ISAIAH 26:3-4)

Day Date Scripture

Day Date Scripture

Day Date Scripture

Day Date Scripture

Day Date Scripture

Day Date Scripture

Day Date Scripture

Special Notes

Prayer List

PRAYER POINT:

Your Whole House Shall Be Saved

INSPIRATIONAL QUOTE

"Salvation may be personal, but it's still a promise for your entire household."
Teresa Wilson

Acts 16:31

They replied, "Believe in the Lord Jesus, and you will be saved - you and your household.

Prayer

Father, in the name of Jesus, I declare that the promise of Salvation has come to my entire house. I declare that my entire family is born again and Spirit filled. I declare that all spiritual blindness has been removed and the power of God is made manifest to them. I declare that my whole house shall be saved. I plead the Blood of Jesus over every member in my family. In Jesus' name, Amen.

www.teresabwilson.com

Weekly Devotions

YOU KEEP HIM IN PERFECT PEACE WHOSE MIND IS STAYED ON YOU, BECAUSE HE TRUSTS IN YOU. TRUST IN THE LORD FOREVER, FOR THE LORD GOD IS AN EVERLASTING ROCK. (ISAIAH 26:3-4)

Day Date Scripture

Day Date Scripture

Day Date Scripture

Day Date Scripture

Day Date Scripture

Day Date Scripture

Day Date Scripture

Special Notes

Prayer List

PRAYER POINT:

Anxiety

Inspirational Quotes

"Anxiety does not empty tomorrow of its sorrows, but only empties today of its strength."
Charles Spurgeon

Phillipians 4:6-7

Be anxious for nothing, but in everything by prayer and supplication,
with thanksgiving, let your requests be made known to God; and the peace of God, which passes all understanding, will guard your hearts and minds through Christ Jesus.

Prayer

Father, I come to you in the name of Jesus, casting all my cares upon You, because You care for me. Let not my heart be troubled, and let the peace of God rule in my heart. You will keep me in perfect peace, whose mind is stayed on you because I trust in you. In the name of Jesus, Amen

Weekly Devotions

YOU KEEP HIM IN PERFECT PEACE WHOSE MIND IS STAYED ON YOU, BECAUSE HE TRUSTS IN YOU. TRUST IN THE LORD FOREVER, FOR THE LORD GOD IS AN EVERLASTING ROCK. (ISAIAH 26:3-4)

Day Date Scripture

Day Date Scripture

Day Date Scripture

Day Date Scripture

Day Date Scripture

Day Date Scripture

Day Date Scripture

Special Notes

Prayer List

PRAYER POINT:

Depression

INSPIRATIONAL QUOTES

"A positive attitude gives you power over your circumstances instead of your circumstances having power over you."
Joyce Meyer

Philippians 4:8

Finally, brethren, whatever things are true, whatever things are noble, whatever things are just, whatever things are pure, whatever things are lovely, whatever things are of good report, if there is any virtue and if there is anything praiseworthy - meditate on these things.

Prayer

Father, You have good thoughts and good plans for me. Plans to prosper me and give me hope and a future. You keep me in perfect peace, peace of mind and heart. Father, I receive a spirit of power, love, and a calm and well-balanced mind with discipline and self-control, which You have given me. I loose self-defeating thought patterns from my mind. I tear down strongholds that have protected bad perceptions about myself. I will not give the devil a way to defeat me by harboring resentment, holding onto self-hatred, anger toward myself and others, or feeling guilty. I will cooperate with the Holy Spirit who is helping me renew my thoughts and attitudes with Your Word. In Jesus' name, Amen

Weekly Devotions

YOU KEEP HIM IN PERFECT PEACE WHOSE MIND IS STAYED ON YOU, BECAUSE HE TRUSTS IN YOU. TRUST IN THE LORD FOREVER, FOR THE LORD GOD IS AN EVERLASTING ROCK. (ISAIAH 26:3-4)

Day Date Scripture

Day Date Scripture

Day Date Scripture

Day Date Scripture

Day Date Scripture

Day Date Scripture

Day Date Scripture

Special Notes

Prayer List

PRAYER POINT:

Favor

INSPIRATIONAL QUOTE

"You did not earn this honor or favor. It was given to you by God. Jesus earned it for you."
— Dr. Bill Winston

Job 10:12

You have granted me life and favor,
and Your providence has preserved my spirit.

Prayer

I declare and decree favor over my life. Favor surrounds me everywhere I go. By Your favor O Lord, You have established me as a strong mountain. Thank You, for you are the glory of my strength. I will continue to expect great things to come my way. In Jesus' name, Amen.

Weekly Devotions

YOU KEEP HIM IN PERFECT PEACE WHOSE MIND IS STAYED ON YOU, BECAUSE HE TRUSTS IN YOU. TRUST IN THE LORD FOREVER, FOR THE LORD GOD IS AN EVERLASTING ROCK. (ISAIAH 26:3-4)

Day Date Scripture

Day Date Scripture

Day Date Scripture

Day Date Scripture

Day Date Scripture

Day Date Scripture

Day Date Scripture

Special Notes

Prayer List

PRAYER POINT:

Power In The Blood

INSPIRATIONAL QUOTE

"The Blood of Jesus washes away our past and the name of Jesus opens up our future."
Jesse Duplantis

Exodus 12:7

And they shall take of the blood, and strike it on the two side posts and on the upper door post of the houses, wherein they shall eat it.

Prayer

From Joyce Meyer: The Word the Name the Blood

Father, I declare the blood of Jesus over my life and all that belongs to me. The Blood of Jesus covers my mind, my emotions, my will, and my body. I am protected by the blood of the Lamb which gives me access to the Most Holy Place - Your Presence. I declare the blood over the places where my children, my grandchildren and their children dwell, and on all those whom You have given me in this life. Lord you have said that the life of the body is in the blood. I'm so thankful for the blood of Jesus that has cleansed me from sin and has begun the eternal agreement with Your people, the New Covenant, of which I am a part. In Jesus' Name, Amen.

Weekly Devotions

YOU KEEP HIM IN PERFECT PEACE WHOSE MIND IS STAYED ON YOU, BECAUSE HE TRUSTS IN YOU. TRUST IN THE LORD FOREVER, FOR THE LORD GOD IS AN EVERLASTING ROCK. (ISAIAH 26:3-4)

Day ___ Date ___ Scripture ___

Day ___ Date ___ Scripture ___

Day ___ Date ___ Scripture ___

Day ___ Date ___ Scripture ___

Day ___ Date ___ Scripture ___

Day ___ Date ___ Scripture ___

Day ___ Date ___ Scripture ___

Special Notes

Prayer List

PRAYER POINT:

God's Image – My Image

INSPIRATIONAL QUOTE

"As you begin changing your thinking, start immediately to change your behavior. Begin to act the part of the person you would like to become. Take action on your behavior. Too many people want to feel, then take action. This never works."
John Maxwell

Romans 4:17

(As it is written, I have made thee a father of many nations,) before him whom he believed, even God, who quickened the dead, and called those things which be not as though they were.

Prayer

Father, Your word says to strip myself of my former nature (put off and discard my old unrenewed self) which characterized my previous manner of life. I am constantly being renewed in the spirit of my mind (having a fresh mental and spiritual attitude), and I put on the new nature (the regenerate self) created in God's image, (Godlike) in true righteousness and holiness. Thank You for Your word that is truth. I am who You say I am. In Jesus' name, Amen.

Weekly Devotions

YOU KEEP HIM IN PERFECT PEACE WHOSE MIND IS STAYED ON YOU, BECAUSE HE TRUSTS IN YOU. TRUST IN THE LORD FOREVER, FOR THE LORD GOD IS AN EVERLASTING ROCK. (ISAIAH 26:3-4)

Day ___ Date ___ Scripture ___

Day ___ Date ___ Scripture ___

Day ___ Date ___ Scripture ___

Day ___ Date ___ Scripture ___

Day ___ Date ___ Scripture ___

Day ___ Date ___ Scripture ___

Day ___ Date ___ Scripture ___

Special Notes

Prayer List

PRAYER POINT:

Authority

Inspirational Quotes

"Your words open & close the door to the enemy and his work in the earth. Use your authorit to put the devil in place."
Joyce Meyer

Luke 10:19

Behold! I have given you the authority to trample on serpents and scorpions, and over all the power of the enemy, and nothing shall by any means hurt you.... You have the authority of Almighty God!

Prayer

Father, in the name of Jesus, as a disciple of Christ, I have the keys of the Kingdom of heaven; whatever I bind on earth is bound, and whatever I loose is loosed. I use the sword of the spirit to active the kingdom You have freely given to me. I put the devil in his place. I command him to stay away from my family, my finances, and everything that I own. If God is for me, who can be against me? In Jesus' name, Amen.

Weekly Devotions

YOU KEEP HIM IN PERFECT PEACE WHOSE MIND IS STAYED ON YOU, BECAUSE HE TRUSTS IN YOU. TRUST IN THE LORD FOREVER, FOR THE LORD GOD IS AN EVERLASTING ROCK. (ISAIAH 26:3-4)

Day Date Scripture

Special Notes

Day Date Scripture

Day Date Scripture

Day Date Scripture

Prayer List

Day Date Scripture

Day Date Scripture

Day Date Scripture

PRAYER POINT:

Prejudice

INSPIRATIONAL QUOTE

"Darkness cannot drive out darkness; only light can do that. Hate cannot drive out hate; only Love can do that."
Dr. Martin Luther King Jr.

Ephesians 4:1-6

Therefore I, a prisoner for serving the Lord, beg you to lead a life worthy of your calling, for you have been called by God. Be humble and gentle. Be patient with each other, making allowance for each other's faults because of your love. Always keep yourselves united in the Holy Spirit, and bind yourselves together with peace. We are all one body, we have the same Spirit and we have all been called to the same glorious future. There is only one Lord, one faith, one baptism, and there is only one God and Father, who is over us all and in us all and living through us all.

Prayer

Father, in the name of Jesus, I come before You, asking Your forgiveness for being intolerant of others because of the color of their skin. Forgive me for tolerating prejudice in the church. Set me free from the influence of public opinion that I may live out my glorious faith. We are one blood. We were bought with blood that is worth much - the blood of Christ. I pray for an end to division in Christ's family. All of us are equal - slave and free, male and female. We are all in a common relationship with Jesus Christ. The Kingdom of Faith is now our home country. In Jesus' name, Amen.

Weekly Devotions

YOU KEEP HIM IN PERFECT PEACE WHOSE MIND IS STAYED ON YOU, BECAUSE HE TRUSTS IN YOU. TRUST IN THE LORD FOREVER, FOR THE LORD GOD IS AN EVERLASTING ROCK. (ISAIAH 26:3-4)

Day Date Scripture

Special Notes

Day Date Scripture

Day Date Scripture

Day Date Scripture

Prayer List

Day Date Scripture

Day Date Scripture

Day Date Scripture

PRAYER POINT:

Life

Inspirational Quote

"Speak God's words over your circumstances today. Speak His words in faith and watch Him move!"
Kenneth Copeland

Mark 11:23

For assuredly, I say to you, whoever says to this mountain, "Be removed and be cast into the sea," and does not doubt in his heart, but believes that those things he says will be done, he will have whatever he says.

Prayer

In the name of Jesus, the name above all names that every knee shall bow to, I thank You. For whatever I ask for in prayer shall be done. Heaven backs me up. Angels are waiting for me to activate Your word. I use the authority You have given me to speak life into my circumstances. I will continue to keep Your truth, Your word in my heart. Thank You for all of Your promises for they are yes and amen. In Jesus Name, Amen.

Weekly Devotions

YOU KEEP HIM IN PERFECT PEACE WHOSE MIND IS STAYED ON YOU, BECAUSE HE TRUSTS IN YOU. TRUST IN THE LORD FOREVER, FOR THE LORD GOD IS AN EVERLASTING ROCK. (ISAIAH 26:3-4)

Day Date Scripture

Day Date Scripture

Day Date Scripture

Day Date Scripture

Day Date Scripture

Day Date Scripture

Day Date Scripture

Special Notes

Prayer List

PRAYER POINT:

Armor of God

INSPIRATIONAL QUOTE

"When your faith is the strongest, you come up under the greatest attack, because the enemy is trying to detour your destiny."
~ T. D. Jakes

Ephesians 6:10-18

Finally, be strong in the Lord and in his mighty power. Put on the full armor of God, so that you can take your stand against the devil's schemes. For our struggle is not against flesh and blood, but against the rulers, against the authorities, against the powers of this dark world and against the spiritual forces of evil in the heavenly realms. Therefore put on the full armor of God, so that when the day of evil comes, you may be able to stand your ground, and after you have done everything, to stand. Stand firm then, with the belt of truth buckled around your waist, with the breastplate of righteousness in place, and with your feet fitted with the readiness that comes from the

gospel of peace. In addition to all this, take up the shield of faith, with which you can extinguish all the flaming arrows of the evil one. Take the helmet of salvation and the sword of the Spirit, which is the word of God.
And pray in the Spirit on all occasions with all kinds of prayers and requests. With this in mind, be alert and always keep on praying for all the Lord's people.

Prayer

In the name of Jesus, I put on the full armor of God, so that I am able to stand firm against the strategies of the enemy. I put on the belt of truth and continue to believe in the Word of God. I put on the breastplate of righteousness, knowing that I am in right standing with God. I put on and be ready with the gospel of peace, for Jesus is peace. I hold on to the shield of faith to stop all those fiery darts. I put on the helmet of salvation and remind myself I have the mind of Christ, and I use the sword of the spirit which is the word of God to speak life. In Jesus' name, Amen.

Weekly Devotions

YOU KEEP HIM IN PERFECT PEACE WHOSE MIND IS STAYED ON YOU, BECAUSE HE TRUSTS IN YOU. TRUST IN THE LORD FOREVER, FOR THE LORD GOD IS AN EVERLASTING ROCK. (ISAIAH 26:3-4)

Day	Date	Scripture	Special Notes
Day	Date	Scripture	
Day	Date	Scripture	
Day	Date	Scripture	Prayer List
Day	Date	Scripture	
Day	Date	Scripture	
Day	Date	Scripture	

PRAYER POINT:

Hopelessness

Inspirational Quotes

"The life in front of you is far more important than the life behind you."
Joel Osteen

Psalm 56:3-4,8

But when I am afraid, I will put my trust in You. I praise God, so why should I be afraid? You keep track of all my sorrows. You have collected all my tears in Your bottle. You have recorded each one in Your book.

Prayer

Father, I give You all my worries and cares. I am well balanced, cautious, and alert watching out for the attacks of the enemy. I am confident I will see Your goodness. In the name of Jesus, I gain the victory by the blood of the Lamb and by the word of my witness. In Jesus' name, Amen.

Weekly Devotions

YOU KEEP HIM IN PERFECT PEACE WHOSE MIND IS STAYED ON YOU, BECAUSE HE TRUSTS IN YOU. TRUST IN THE LORD FOREVER, FOR THE LORD GOD IS AN EVERLASTING ROCK. (ISAIAH 26:3-4)

Day Date Scripture

Special Notes

Day Date Scripture

Day Date Scripture

Day Date Scripture

Prayer List

Day Date Scripture

Day Date Scripture

Day Date Scripture

PRAYER POINT:

Draw Close to God

Inspirational Quotes

"The only way to draw near to God is to spend quiet time with Him."
Teresa Wilson

James 4:8

Draw near to God and He will draw near to you. Cleanse your hands, you sinners; and purify your hearts, you double-minded.

Prayer

God, be Lord of my life today. Have total and complete control. Take my heart for Your own. I bow to You, Lord

Jesus. I acknowledge You as my Lord and King. Let Your word increase in my life, and set a watch over my mouth. Let my mouth stay shut when I'm even tempted to say anything that is not from You. Most of all, give me wisdom. Make me like You. Conform me to the image of Christ. Help me develop Godly character. In Jesus' name, Amen.

www.teresabwilson.com

Weekly Devotions

YOU KEEP HIM IN PERFECT PEACE WHOSE MIND IS STAYED ON YOU, BECAUSE HE TRUSTS IN YOU. TRUST IN THE LORD FOREVER, FOR THE LORD GOD IS AN EVERLASTING ROCK. (ISAIAH 26:3-4)

Day Date Scripture

Special Notes

Day Date Scripture

Day Date Scripture

Day Date Scripture

Prayer List

Day Date Scripture

Day Date Scripture

Day Date Scripture

PRAYER POINT:

Emotional Healing

INSPIRATIONAL QUOTE

"You can suffer the pain of change or suffer remaining the way you are."
Joyce Meyer

Isaiah 61:3

To appoint unto them that mourn in Zion, to give unto them beauty for ashes, the oil of joy for mourning, the garment of praise for the spirit of heaviness; that they might be called trees of righteousness, the planting of the Lord, that he might be glorified.

Prayer

God, I thank you for Your goodness and grace toward me. I declare that I have received beauty in exchange for ashes. I declare that I am a tree of righteousness. I declare that I am planted in Your kingdom. I declare that despair, depression, and rejection no longer operate in my life. I choose to rejoice in Your goodness. I will praise You all of my days. In the name of Jesus, Amen.

Weekly Devotions

YOU KEEP HIM IN PERFECT PEACE WHOSE MIND IS STAYED ON YOU, BECAUSE HE TRUSTS IN YOU. TRUST IN THE LORD FOREVER, FOR THE LORD GOD IS AN EVERLASTING ROCK. (ISAIAH 26:3-4)

Day Date Scripture

Special Notes

Day Date Scripture

Day Date Scripture

Day Date Scripture

Prayer List

Day Date Scripture

Day Date Scripture

Day Date Scripture

PRAYER POINT:

Overcome Procrastination

Inspirational Quote

My advice is to never do tomorrow what you can do today. Procrastination is the thief of time.
~ Charles Dickens

Proverbs 10:4

A slack hand causes poverty, but the hand of the diligent makes rich.

Prayer

Father, I know that I am a procrastinator. I understand now that by procrastinating

I am not living the abundant life You want for me, and for this I am sorry.
I ask, Father, that you forgive me for delays which have led to disobedience. Forgive me for letting fear stand in my way, forgive me for idleness and for any other reason I may not be aware of. Help me to confront them honestly so that I may overcome.
Father, help me to hear Your voice daily so that I may act in accordance with Your will. I ask for courage where there is fear to overcome laziness, and idleness. Today I choose to walk Your path in discernment, courage and conviction.
In Jesus' name, Amen.

Weekly Devotions

YOU KEEP HIM IN PERFECT PEACE WHOSE MIND IS STAYED ON YOU, BECAUSE HE TRUSTS IN YOU. TRUST IN THE LORD FOREVER, FOR THE LORD GOD IS AN EVERLASTING ROCK. (ISAIAH 26:3-4)

Day Date Scripture

Day Date Scripture

Day Date Scripture

Day Date Scripture

Day Date Scripture

Day Date Scripture

Day Date Scripture

Special Notes

Prayer List

PRAYER POINT:

Go Of The Past

INSPIRATIONAL QUOTES

Don't let fear or past disappointmentshold you back.
~Kenneth Copeland

Proverbs 4:25

Let your eyes look straight ahead;
fix your gaze directly before you.

Prayer

Father, in the name of Jesus, I have been crucified with Christ and I no longer live, but Christ lives in me. The life I now live in the body, I live by Faith in the Son of God. One thing that I will do just like Paul is forgetting what is behind me, and straining toward what is ahead. I will press on toward the goal, to win the prize for which God has called me in Christ Jesus. Amen.

Weekly Devotions

YOU KEEP HIM IN PERFECT PEACE WHOSE MIND IS STAYED ON YOU, BECAUSE HE TRUSTS IN YOU. TRUST IN THE LORD FOREVER, FOR THE LORD GOD IS AN EVERLASTING ROCK. (ISAIAH 26:3-4)

Day Date Scripture

Day Date Scripture

Day Date Scripture

Day Date Scripture

Day Date Scripture

Day Date Scripture

Day Date Scripture

Special Notes

Prayer List

PRAYER POINT:

Have Faith In God

INSPIRATIONAL QUOTES

"When you speak the Word of God over your situations, that's when you put your Faith to work!"
~ Bill Winston

Hebrews 4:12

For the Word of God is alive and active. Sharper than any double-edged sword, it penetrates even to dividing soul and spirit, joints and marrow; it judges the thoughts and attitudes of the heart

Prayer

Father, Your word says that without faith it is impossible to please You. Therefore, I active Your word over my family, finances, and everything that I own. All of my needs are met, I lack nothing. I am protected by Your blood and no sickness or diseases come near me. Everything I put my hands to will prosper. Everything that I touch is blessed. I speak life over all of my circumstances as I walk by faith and not by what I see. In Jesus' name, Amen.

Weekly Devotions

YOU KEEP HIM IN PERFECT PEACE WHOSE MIND IS STAYED ON YOU, BECAUSE HE TRUSTS IN YOU. TRUST IN THE LORD FOREVER, FOR THE LORD GOD IS AN EVERLASTING ROCK. (ISAIAH 26:3-4)

Day Date Scripture

Day Date Scripture

Day Date Scripture

Day Date Scripture

Day Date Scripture

Day Date Scripture

Day Date Scripture

Special Notes

Prayer List

PRAYER POINT:

Humility

INSPIRATIONAL QUOTE

"Pray that God will impart to you a deeper revelation of all He wants you to accomplish and that you will have unshakeable faith in Him!"
~ Sid Roth

Proverbs 16:18

Pride goes before destruction, and haughtiness before a fall.

Prayer

Father, I humble myself before You. Check my heart and my motives. Show me if there is any pride creeping in. I will depend on You and only You. Help me to set my heart and my mind on

the things of God. Help me to walk
in humility. Continue to teach me Your
ways as I grow in you day by day. Thank
you for never giving up on me. In the name of Jesus, Amen.

Weekly Devotions

YOU KEEP HIM IN PERFECT PEACE WHOSE MIND IS STAYED ON YOU, BECAUSE HE TRUSTS IN YOU. TRUST IN THE LORD FOREVER, FOR THE LORD GOD IS AN EVERLASTING ROCK. (ISAIAH 26:3-4)

Day   Date   Scripture

Day   Date   Scripture

Day   Date   Scripture

Day   Date   Scripture

Day   Date   Scripture

Day   Date   Scripture

Day   Date   Scripture

Special Notes

Prayer List

PRAYER POINT:

Blessed

INSPIRATIONAL QUOTE

"Talk about your blessings more than your burdens."~ Terri Savelle Foy

Psalm 34:8

Taste and see that the Lord is good;
blessed is the one who takes refuge in him.

Prayer

Father, in the name of Jesus, I thank You for Your word. Your word is truth. I fix my thoughts and declare with my mouth that I lack nothing. I am blessed coming in and blessed going out. Your word does not come back void. Thank You for Your promises, that they are all yes and Amen. Glory be to God. In Jesus' name, Amen

Weekly Devotions

YOU KEEP HIM IN PERFECT PEACE WHOSE MIND IS STAYED ON YOU, BECAUSE HE TRUSTS IN YOU. TRUST IN THE LORD FOREVER, FOR THE LORD GOD IS AN EVERLASTING ROCK. (ISAIAH 26:3-4)

Day Date Scripture

Day Date Scripture

Day Date Scripture

Day Date Scripture

Day Date Scripture

Day Date Scripture

Day Date Scripture

Special Notes

Prayer List

PRAYER POINT:

Gratitude

INSPIRATIONAL QUOTE

"God moves in an atmosphere of gratitude"
~Terri Savelle Foy

1 Thessalonians 5:16-18

Rejoice always, pray continually, give thanks in all circumstances; for this is God's will for you in Christ Jesus.

Prayer

Father, I am so grateful and thankful for all Your goodness. Thank You, for Your grace and mercy are new every morning. Thank You for being my Jehovah-Jireh, the Lord that provides. I am grateful for walking, I am grateful for my arms and legs, and all the little things that I so take advantage of. Thank You that You always lead me and guide me. Thank You for never leaving me. In Jesus' name, Amen.

Weekly Devotions

YOU KEEP HIM IN PERFECT PEACE WHOSE MIND IS STAYED ON YOU, BECAUSE HE TRUSTS IN YOU. TRUST IN THE LORD FOREVER, FOR THE LORD GOD IS AN EVERLASTING ROCK. (ISAIAH 26:3-4)

Day Date Scripture

Special Notes

Day Date Scripture

Day Date Scripture

Day Date Scripture

Prayer List

Day Date Scripture

Day Date Scripture

Day Date Scripture

PRAYER POINT:

Spiritual Hunger

INSPIRATIONAL QUOTE

"You do the natural. Trust God for the super."
~Steven Furtick

Matthew 5:6

Blessed are they which do hunger and thirst after righteousness: for they shall be filled.

Prayer

Father, in the name of Jesus, thank You for Your unfailing Word. I declare a supernatural hunger and thirst for Your word in my life. Your word says blessed are those who hunger and thirst after righteousness for they shall be filled.
I declare for a spiritual awakening in my life, I pray this over my spouse, over my children, and

over my loved ones. I am filled with the fullness of Almighty God. In Jesus' name, Amen.

Weekly Devotions

YOU KEEP HIM IN PERFECT PEACE WHOSE MIND IS STAYED ON YOU, BECAUSE HE TRUSTS IN YOU. TRUST IN THE LORD FOREVER, FOR THE LORD GOD IS AN EVERLASTING ROCK. (ISAIAH 26:3-4)

Day   Date   Scripture

Special Notes

Day   Date   Scripture

Day   Date   Scripture

Day   Date   Scripture

Prayer List

Day   Date   Scripture

Day   Date   Scripture

Day   Date   Scripture

PRAYER POINT:

Selfish

INSPIRATIONAL QUOTE

"We manifest character when self-sacrifice for the sake of our principles becomes more important than compromise for the sake of popularity."
~Myles Monroe

1 Corinthians 10:24

I must not think only of myself but try to think of the other fellow, too, and what is best for him.

Prayer

Father, in the name of Jesus, I will love others with brotherly affection, giving precedence and showing honor to them. I make it a practice to please my neighbor for his good and for his true welfare, to edify him to strengthen him and build him up spiritually. I am blessed and I am a blessing to people. Christ died for all, so that all those who live might live no longer to and for themselves, but to and for Him who died and was raised again for their sake. In Jesus' Name, Amen.

Weekly Devotions

YOU KEEP HIM IN PERFECT PEACE WHOSE MIND IS STAYED ON YOU. BECAUSE HE TRUSTS IN YOU. TRUST IN THE LORD FOREVER, FOR THE LORD GOD IS AN EVERLASTING ROCK. (ISAIAH 26:3-4)

Day Date Scripture

Special Notes

Day Date Scripture

Day Date Scripture

Day Date Scripture

Prayer List

Day Date Scripture

Day Date Scripture

Day Date Scripture

PRAYER POINT:

Be Of Good Courage

INSPIRATIONAL QUOTES

"God can turn your failures into a foundation for your future."
~ Steven Furtick

Deuteronomy 31:6

Be strong and courageous. Don't be afraid or scared of them; for the Lord your God Himself is who goes with you. He will not fail you nor forsake you.

Prayer

Father, in the name of Jesus, I declare that I am surrounded by an entire host of angelic armies. You give Your angels charge over me to keep me in all of my ways. I declare that I will not be overtaken by fear, anxiety, worry, or terror in the name of Jesus. Thank You that You are for me and not against me. Thank you for loving me.
In Jesus' Name, Amen.

Weekly Devotions

YOU KEEP HIM IN PERFECT PEACE WHOSE MIND IS STAYED ON YOU, BECAUSE HE TRUSTS IN YOU. TRUST IN THE LORD FOREVER, FOR THE LORD GOD IS AN EVERLASTING ROCK. (ISAIAH 26:3-4)

Day   Date   Scripture

Day   Date   Scripture

Day   Date   Scripture

Day   Date   Scripture

Day   Date   Scripture

Day   Date   Scripture

Day   Date   Scripture

Special Notes

Prayer List

PRAYER POINT:

Worship Him

INSPIRATIONAL QUOTES

*"Happy moments, PRAISE GOD.
Difficult moments, SEEK GOD.
Quit moments, WORSHIP GOD.
Painful moments, TRUST GOD.
Every moment. THANK GOD."
~Rick Warren*

Psalm 119:38

The Lord establishes His word and confirms His promise to me. He is for those who reverently fear and devotedly worship Him.

~ Prayer ~

I will bless the Lord at all times; His praise shall continually be in my mouth. I will lift up my hands in Your name. My soul shall be satisfied as with marrow and fatness, and my mouth shall praise You with joyful lips, because of Your lovingkindness is better than life, My lips shall praise You. I will bless You while I live. In the name of Jesus, Amen.

Weekly Devotions

YOU KEEP HIM IN PERFECT PEACE WHOSE MIND IS STAYED ON YOU, BECAUSE HE TRUSTS IN YOU. TRUST IN THE LORD FOREVER, FOR THE LORD GOD IS AN EVERLASTING ROCK. (ISAIAH 26:3-4)

Day Date Scripture

Day Date Scripture

Day Date Scripture

Day Date Scripture

Day Date Scripture

Day Date Scripture

Day Date Scripture

Special Notes

Prayer List

PRAYER POINT:

Identity

Inspirational Quote

"Fill your mind with God's word and you will have no room for Satan's lies."
Anonymous

Proverbs 23:7

For as he thinks in his heart,
so is he.....

Prayer

Father, I can not have a positive life with a negative mind. The Lord guards me, He keeps me in perfect and constant peace because my mind is stayed on Him. I commit myself in You, lean on You, and hope confidently in You. In quietness and

in trusting confidence I find strength.
In Jesus' name, Amen.

Weekly Devotions

YOU KEEP HIM IN PERFECT PEACE WHOSE MIND IS STAYED ON YOU, BECAUSE HE TRUSTS IN YOU. TRUST IN THE LORD FOREVER, FOR THE LORD GOD IS AN EVERLASTING ROCK. (ISAIAH 26:3-4)

Day Date Scripture

Day Date Scripture

Day Date Scripture

Day Date Scripture

Day Date Scripture

Day Date Scripture

Day Date Scripture

Special Notes

Prayer List

PRAYER POINT:

Strengthen The Inner Man

INSPIRATIONAL QUOTE

"We can be tired, weary and emotionally distraught, but after spending time alone with God, we find that He injects into our bodies energy, power and strength." - Charles Stanley

Isaiah 50:4

The Sovereign Lord has given me His words of wisdom, so that I know what to say to all these weary ones. Morning by morning He awakens me and opens my understanding to His will.

Prayer

Father, I thank You for Your miraculous power in my spirit, soul, and body. Thank You for the revelation of the Holy Spirit in my inner being, which is producing in me a desire to do what is pleasing in Your sight. I thank You for Your power and might working in me. I know that it is Your will for me to always flourish. I declare that I am spiritually alert and aware of Your presence. Thank You for awakening me morning by morning and opening up my understanding to Your will. In Jesus' name, Amen.

Weekly Devotions

YOU KEEP HIM IN PERFECT PEACE WHOSE MIND IS STAYED ON YOU, BECAUSE HE TRUSTS IN YOU. TRUST IN THE LORD FOREVER, FOR THE LORD GOD IS AN EVERLASTING ROCK. (ISAIAH 26:3-4)

Day Date Scripture

Special Notes

Day Date Scripture

Day Date Scripture

Day Date Scripture

Prayer List

Day Date Scripture

Day Date Scripture

Day Date Scripture

PRAYER POINT:

God's Love

INSPIRATIONAL QUOTE

"Life is too short, the world is too big and God's love is too great to live ordinary."
Christine Caine

Romans 5:5

And hope maketh not ashamed; because the love of God is shed abroad in our hearts by the Holy Ghost which is given unto us. For we know how dearly God loves us, because He has given us the Holy Spirit to fill our hearts with His love

Prayer

Father, in the name of Jesus, thank You for loving me, for filling my heart with love by the Holy Spirit. I am Your child and I commit to walk in Your love. I will keep and treasure Your word. In Jesus name. Amen.

Weekly Devotions

YOU KEEP HIM IN PERFECT PEACE WHOSE MIND IS STAYED ON YOU, BECAUSE HE TRUSTS IN YOU. TRUST IN THE LORD FOREVER, FOR THE LORD GOD IS AN EVERLASTING ROCK. (ISAIAH 26:3-4)

Day Date Scripture

Day Date Scripture

Day Date Scripture

Day Date Scripture

Day Date Scripture

Day Date Scripture

Day Date Scripture

Special Notes

Prayer List

PRAYER POINT:

A Life Turned Around

INSPIRATIONAL QUOTE

"We have so many Christians who want to change the world, but they don't want to change themselves."
~ Christine Caine

Ephesians 5;26

So that He might sanctify her, having cleansed her by the washing of water with the word.

Prayer

Lord, when all is lost, I thank You that You reach out to me with Your mighty hand of rescue, that You wash me and cleanse my heart with Your word. If I have allowed the world's viewpoint to diminish who You are, let me now see the truth. Reveal to me where I need change. I can't do this without You, Holy Spirit. I need you. In Jesus' name, Amen.

Weekly Devotions

YOU KEEP HIM IN PERFECT PEACE WHOSE MIND IS STAYED ON YOU, BECAUSE HE TRUSTS IN YOU. TRUST IN THE LORD FOREVER, FOR THE LORD GOD IS AN EVERLASTING ROCK. (ISAIAH 26:3-4)

Day Date Scripture

Special Notes

Day Date Scripture

Day Date Scripture

Day Date Scripture

Prayer List

Day Date Scripture

Day Date Scripture

Day Date Scripture

PRAYER POINT:

Grace

Inspirational Quote

"God doesn't owe us anything. Yet in His grace, He still gives us good things."
~Billy Graham

Titus 2:11-12

For the grace of God has appeared that offers salvation to all people. It teaches us to say "No" to ungodliness and worldly passions, and to live self-controlled, upright and godly lives in this present age.

Prayer

Father, I am so thankful for Your grace, Your word says that You have granted me life and favor and Your care has preserved my spirit. To the praise of the glory of His grace, by which He made us accepted in the beloved. So let us come boldly to the throne of grace, that we may obtain mercy and find grace to help in time of need. In Jesus' name, Amen.

PRAYER POINT:

Purpose

INSPIRATIONAL QUOTE

"Success is always the result of following the leading of the Holy Spirit"
~Kenneth E. Hagin

~Jeremiah 29:11~

For I know the plans I have for you, says the Lord. "They are plans for good and not for disaster, to give you a future and a hope.

~Prayer~

Father, thank You for Your plans. Your plans are for good and not for disaster. I will remind myself that when negativity comes my way, it is not from You. You are a good Father. Lead me, Holy Spirit, into purpose in my life. You have given me gifts and talents for Your glory. I will continue to worship You and spend time with You. In Jesus name, Amen.

Weekly Devotions

YOU KEEP HIM IN PERFECT PEACE WHOSE MIND IS STAYED ON YOU, BECAUSE HE TRUSTS IN YOU. TRUST IN THE LORD FOREVER, FOR THE LORD GOD IS AN EVERLASTING ROCK. (ISAIAH 26:3-4)

Day Date Scripture

Day Date Scripture

Day Date Scripture

Day Date Scripture

Day Date Scripture

Day Date Scripture

Day Date Scripture

Special Notes

Prayer List

PRAYER POINT:

Insecurity

INSPIRATIONAL QUOTE

"Don't be afraid of your flaws; acknowledge them and let God use you anyway. Quit worrying about what you're not and give God what you are."
~John Hagee

Psalm 27:1

The Lord is my Light and my Salvation whom shall I fear or dread? The Lord is the Refuge and Stronghold of my life of whom shall I be afraid?

Insecurity

Lord, I pray over my heart. I ask that You would continue to transform me. When insecurities flare up, they take over my whole heart and mind. I dwell on the negative and not the positive. May Your Holy Spirit comfort me and train me to see life from Your perspective. Lord, I am asking you to replace this insecurity With confidence. In Jesus' name, Amen.

Weekly Devotions

YOU KEEP HIM IN PERFECT PEACE WHOSE MIND IS STAYED ON YOU, BECAUSE HE TRUSTS IN YOU. TRUST IN THE LORD FOREVER, FOR THE LORD GOD IS AN EVERLASTING ROCK. (ISAIAH 26:3-4)

Day Date Scripture

Special Notes

Day Date Scripture

Day Date Scripture

Day Date Scripture

Prayer List

Day Date Scripture

Day Date Scripture

Day Date Scripture

PRAYER POINT:

You Are Chosen

INSPIRATIONAL QUOTE

"You are called to shine right where you are!"
~Nicole Crank

⸺ 1 Peter 2;9 ⸺

"But you are a chosen race, a royal priesthood,
a holy nation, a people for his own possession,
that you make proclaim the excellencies of him
who called you out of darkness into
his marvelous
light."

⸺ Prayer ⸺

Lord, I am chosen by You. I am loved by You.
I am rich in every way and generous on every
occasion. I am anointed, appointed, equipped,

and enabled by the power of God that works mightily within me! In Jesus name, Amen.

Weekly Devotions

YOU KEEP HIM IN PERFECT PEACE WHOSE MIND IS STAYED ON YOU, BECAUSE HE TRUSTS IN YOU. TRUST IN THE LORD FOREVER, FOR THE LORD GOD IS AN EVERLASTING ROCK. (ISAIAH 26:3-4)

Day Date Scripture

Day Date Scripture

Day Date Scripture

Day Date Scripture

Day Date Scripture

Day Date Scripture

Day Date Scripture

Special Notes

Prayer List

PRAYER POINT:

Living In The Overflow

INSPIRATIONAL QUOTE

"Stand boldly on the promise that since God is for you, no one an nothing can stand against you!"
Gary Keesee

Proverbs 10:22

The blessing of the Lord makes a person rich, and he adds no sorrow with it.

Prayer

Father, it is Your will for me to live the abundant life for which Jesus died for me.

I declare that Your supernatural power is at work in me. I will enjoy all of the benefits that you have for me. Everything that I put my hand to work shall prosper. I live a victorious life. In Jesus name, Amen.

Weekly Devotions

YOU KEEP HIM IN PERFECT PEACE WHOSE MIND IS STAYED ON YOU, BECAUSE HE TRUSTS IN YOU. TRUST IN THE LORD FOREVER, FOR THE LORD GOD IS AN EVERLASTING ROCK. (ISAIAH 26:3-4)

Day Date Scripture

Special Notes

Day Date Scripture

Day Date Scripture

Day Date Scripture

Prayer List

Day Date Scripture

Day Date Scripture

Day Date Scripture

PRAYER POINT:

You Hold The Key

INSPIRATIONAL QUOTE

"No man can climb beyond the limitations of his own belief."
~Myles Munroe

Matthew 16:19

"I will give you the keys of the kingdom of heaven; whatever you bind on earth will be bound in heaven, and whatever you loose on earth will be loosed in heaven."

Prayer

Father, thank You for the Blood, that I can come boldly to the throne in confidence. That whatever I bind on earth is bound in Heaven, and whatever I loose on earth is loosed in heaven. Thank You for the authority that I have in You. I am the hands and feet of Jesus. I hold the keys to Heaven. I live in abundance. I speak to the mountain and it has to respond. Every knee bows down to the name of Jesus. Amen.

Weekly Devotions

YOU KEEP HIM IN PERFECT PEACE WHOSE MIND IS STAYED ON YOU, BECAUSE HE TRUSTS IN YOU. TRUST IN THE LORD FOREVER, FOR THE LORD GOD IS AN EVERLASTING ROCK. (ISAIAH 26:3-4)

Day   Date   Scripture

Day   Date   Scripture

Day   Date   Scripture

Day   Date   Scripture

Day   Date   Scripture

Day   Date   Scripture

Day   Date   Scripture

Special Notes

Prayer List

PRAYER POINT:

Purify My Heart

Inspirational Quote

"You need to receive the word of God in your heart, not just your head."
Andrew Wommack

2 Corinthians 7:1

Therefore, since we have these promises, dear friends, let us purify ourselves from everything that contaminates body and spirit, perfecting holiness out of reverence of God.

Prayer

Father, I thank You for Your mercy and love toward me. Thank You for Your promises. I declare that my heart is cleansed by the power of Your word. I ask that you forgive me for entertaining thoughts, conversations, and meditations that have affected my heart in a negative way. Remove anything in my heart or mind that is causing spiritual blockage in my life. In Jesus' name, Amen

Weekly Devotions

YOU KEEP HIM IN PERFECT PEACE WHOSE MIND IS STAYED ON YOU, BECAUSE HE TRUSTS IN YOU. TRUST IN THE LORD FOREVER, FOR THE LORD GOD IS AN EVERLASTING ROCK. (ISAIAH 26:3-4)

Day Date Scripture

Special Notes

Day Date Scripture

Day Date Scripture

Day Date Scripture

Prayer List

Day Date Scripture

Day Date Scripture

Day Date Scripture

PRAYER POINT:

Confusion

INSPIRATIONAL QUOTE

*"Everything God does, He does in perfect order.
He is not a God of confusion."*
~John Hagee

1 Corinthians 14:33

For God is not the author of confusion but
of peace, as in all the churches of the saints.

Prayer

Lord, Your word says that if anyone lacks wisdom,
let him ask of God, who gives to all liberally and
without reproach, and it will be given. So I ask
for wisdom. Thank You for not holding back on me.
Thank You for leading me and guiding me. Your word
is a lamp for my feet and a light on my path. I will

be confident in You as You show me the way.
In Jesus' name, Amen.

Weekly Devotions

YOU KEEP HIM IN PERFECT PEACE WHOSE MIND IS STAYED ON YOU, BECAUSE HE TRUSTS IN YOU. TRUST IN THE LORD FOREVER, FOR THE LORD GOD IS AN EVERLASTING ROCK. (ISAIAH 26:3-4)

Day Date Scripture

Special Notes

Day Date Scripture

Day Date Scripture

Day Date Scripture

Prayer List

Day Date Scripture

Day Date Scripture

Day Date Scripture

PRAYER POINT:

Overcoming Your Flaws

INSPIRATIONAL QUOTE

"Don't be afraid of your flaws; acknowledge them and let God use you anyway. Quit worrying about what you're not and give God what you are."
~John Hagee

Psalm 32:8

I will instruct you and teach you in the way you should go; I will guide you with my eye.

Prayer

Father, You are the one who created my inmost being; You

knit me together in my mother's womb. You know the inside and outside of me. I declare that Your goodness and grace is my guide. I open my spiritual eyes to divine opportunities. I am excited about the promises and blessings that You have for me. I declare that I walk in Your miraculous power in every area of my life. In Jesus' name, Amen.

Weekly Devotions

YOU KEEP HIM IN PERFECT PEACE WHOSE MIND IS STAYED ON YOU, BECAUSE HE TRUSTS IN YOU. TRUST IN THE LORD FOREVER, FOR THE LORD GOD IS AN EVERLASTING ROCK. (ISAIAH 26:3-4)

Day Date Scripture

Special Notes

Day Date Scripture

Day Date Scripture

Day Date Scripture

Prayer List

Day Date Scripture

Day Date Scripture

Day Date Scripture

PRAYER POINT:

Hear The Voice Of God

INSPIRATIONAL QUOTE

"We Live in a world of non-stop noise. Do you ever stop long enough hear God?"
Jentezen Franklin

John 10:27

My sheep listen to my voice; I know them, and they follow me.

Prayer

Father, thank You for leading me into my divine purpose. I will pray and read Your word and trust You to speak to my heart to let me know the direction I should go. There is a specific plan for my life. The Holy Spirit can bear witness with my spirit when it comes to making right decisions for my life. In Jesus name, Amen.

Weekly Devotions

YOU KEEP HIM IN PERFECT PEACE WHOSE MIND IS STAYED ON YOU, BECAUSE HE TRUSTS IN YOU. TRUST IN THE LORD FOREVER, FOR THE LORD GOD IS AN EVERLASTING ROCK. (ISAIAH 26:3-4)

Day Date Scripture

Special Notes

Day Date Scripture

Day Date Scripture

Day Date Scripture

Prayer List

Day Date Scripture

Day Date Scripture

Day Date Scripture

PRAYER POINT:

You Already Have It

INSPIRATIONAL QUOTE

"Within you lies the ability to create a world others want to belong to."
~Patricia King

2 Peter 1:3-4

His divine power has given us everything we need for a godly life through our knowledge of Him who called us by His own glory and goodness. Through these He has given us His very great and precious promises so that through them you may participate in the divine nature, having escaped the corruption in the world caused by evil desires.

Prayer

All praise to God, the Father of our Lord Jesus Christ, who has blessed me with every spiritual blessings in the heavenly realms because I am united with Christ. Lord, I pray Your word and activate my faith that it is done and I already have everything I need. All glory to the Most High. Even before You made the world, You loved me and chose me in Christ to be holy and without fault in Your eyes. Praise you Jesus, Amen.

Weekly Devotions

YOU KEEP HIM IN PERFECT PEACE WHOSE MIND IS STAYED ON YOU, BECAUSE HE TRUSTS IN YOU. TRUST IN THE LORD FOREVER, FOR THE LORD GOD IS AN EVERLASTING ROCK. (ISAIAH 26:3-4)

Day Date Scripture

Special Notes

Day Date Scripture

Day Date Scripture

Day Date Scripture

Prayer List

Day Date Scripture

Day Date Scripture

Day Date Scripture

PRAYER POINT:

Determination

INSPIRATIONAL QUOTE

"We don't come to Jesus for a better life. We come to Jesus because He is life."
~John Bevere

Hebrew 12:1-2

Therefore, since we are surround by such a huge crowd of witnesses to the life of faith, let us run with endurance the race that God has set before us.

Prayer

Thank You, Lord, that I have You on my side to run my race. I can't do this without You. I am determined to finish this race. I cannot fail with You by my side. You strengthen me through the battles I face. No weapon formed against me shall prosper. In Jesus' name, Amen.

Weekly Devotions

YOU KEEP HIM IN PERFECT PEACE WHOSE MIND IS STAYED ON YOU, BECAUSE HE TRUSTS IN YOU. TRUST IN THE LORD FOREVER, FOR THE LORD GOD IS AN EVERLASTING ROCK. (ISAIAH 26:3-4)

Day Date Scripture

Special Notes

Day Date Scripture

Day Date Scripture

Day Date Scripture

Prayer List

Day Date Scripture

Day Date Scripture

Day Date Scripture

PRAYER POINT:

See Through Your Spiritual Eyes

Inspirational Quote

"The battle is not against who we have been, it is all-out war against who we are becoming."
~Lisa Bevere

Ephesians 1:18

Having the eyes of your hearts enlightened, that you may know what is the hope to which he has called you, what are the riches of his glorious inheritance in the saints.

Prayer

Every area in my life is blessed because of the light of Your Word shining in and through it. I declare that I will no longer yield to deception, falsehood. or wickedness in any area in my life. I declare that, from this day forward, I will see You in the way the Word of God reveals You. In Jesus' name, Amen.

Weekly Devotions

YOU KEEP HIM IN PERFECT PEACE WHOSE MIND IS STAYED ON YOU, BECAUSE HE TRUSTS IN YOU. TRUST IN THE LORD FOREVER, FOR THE LORD GOD IS AN EVERLASTING ROCK. (ISAIAH 26:3-4)

Day Date Scripture   Special Notes

Day Date Scripture

Day Date Scripture

Day Date Scripture   Prayer List

Day Date Scripture

Day Date Scripture

Day Date Scripture

PRAYER POINT:

Decree And Declare

INSPIRATIONAL QUOTE

"Program abundance and success into your life every single morning."
~Cindy Trimm

Job 22:28

Thou shalt also decree a thing and it shall be established unto thee: and the light shall shine upon thy ways.

Prayer

I decree the full blessings of Abraham to apprehend me for the rest of my life.

I will live a life of victory I will not look back, but press on to greater things in the spirit every day of my life.
I will speak the word of God with and in the authority that is mine as a child of God.
I will walk with confidence in the destiny of my life for the glory of God.
In Jesus' name, Amen.

Weekly Devotions

YOU KEEP HIM IN PERFECT PEACE WHOSE MIND IS STAYED ON YOU, BECAUSE HE TRUSTS IN YOU. TRUST IN THE LORD FOREVER, FOR THE LORD GOD IS AN EVERLASTING ROCK. (ISAIAH 26:3-4)

Day Date Scripture

Day Date Scripture

Day Date Scripture

Special Notes

Day Date Scripture

Prayer List

Day Date Scripture

Day Date Scripture

Day Date Scripture

PRAYER POINT:

More Than Conquerors

Inspirational Quote

The Kingdom of Light always overpowers the kingdom of darkness.
~John Eckhardt

Romans 8:37

Nay, in all these things we are more than conquerors through Him that loves us.

Prayer

Father, I thank you for the finished work of the cross. I am more than a conqueror through the One who loves me unconditionally. I prophesy to every situation and circumstances in my life and say "Greater is He who lives in me than he that is in the world!" In Jesus' name, Amen.

Weekly Devotions

YOU KEEP HIM IN PERFECT PEACE WHOSE MIND IS STAYED ON YOU. BECAUSE HE TRUSTS IN YOU. TRUST IN THE LORD FOREVER, FOR THE LORD GOD IS AN EVERLASTING ROCK. (ISAIAH 26:3-4)

Day _____ Date _____ Scripture _____

Day _____ Date _____ Scripture _____

Day _____ Date _____ Scripture _____

Day _____ Date _____ Scripture _____

Day _____ Date _____ Scripture _____

Day _____ Date _____ Scripture _____

Day _____ Date _____ Scripture _____

Special Notes

Prayer List

PRAYER POINT:

Deliverance

INSPIRATIONAL QUOTE

"What we do not kill in the spirit will kill us spiritually."
~John Ramirez

Romans 10:9-10

For if you confess with your mouth that Jesus is Lord and believe in your heart that God raised him from the dead, you will be saved. For it is by believing in your heart that you are made right with God, and it is by confessing with your mouth that you are saved.

Prayer

In the name of Jesus, I take authority over any and all forms of emotional bondage, confusion, or turmoil. I declare that I am free from spirits of calamity and chaos. The Word declares that the peace of God rules my heart and mind through Christ Jesus; therefore, I loose myself from the plans and schemes of the evil one. In the name of Jesus, Amen!

Weekly Devotions

YOU KEEP HIM IN PERFECT PEACE WHOSE MIND IS STAYED ON YOU, BECAUSE HE TRUSTS IN YOU. TRUST IN THE LORD FOREVER, FOR THE LORD GOD IS AN EVERLASTING ROCK. (ISAIAH 26:3-4)

Day Date Scripture

Special Notes

Day Date Scripture

Day Date Scripture

Day Date Scripture

Prayer List

Day Date Scripture

Day Date Scripture

Day Date Scripture

PRAYER POINT:

Binding and Loosing

INSPIRATIONAL QUOTE

"Yes, sin, sickness, and disease, spiritual death, poverty and everything else that's of the devil once ruled us. But now, bless God, we rule them-for this is the Day of Dominion!"
~Kenneth Hagin

Matthew 18:18

Verily I say unto you, Whatsoever ye shall bind on earth shall be bound in heaven: and whatsoever ye shall loose on earth shall be loosed in heaven.

Prayer

Father, thank you for the authority and dominion you gave me. I take my stand in the Word of God. I am protected from all harm and evil in Jesus name. I am able to fulfill the calling You have placed in my life. I act in audacious faith to change the world in this generation. I bind the enemy and all his cohorts all his tactics and schemes over my life and my family's life. He can not touch us. I loose wealth, health, peace and the love of God into my life. In Jesus' name, Amen.

Weekly Devotions

YOU KEEP HIM IN PERFECT PEACE WHOSE MIND IS STAYED ON YOU, BECAUSE HE TRUSTS IN YOU. TRUST IN THE LORD FOREVER, FOR THE LORD GOD IS AN EVERLASTING ROCK. (ISAIAH 26:3-4)

Day Date Scripture

Special Notes

Day Date Scripture

Day Date Scripture

Day Date Scripture

Prayer List

Day Date Scripture

Day Date Scripture

Day Date Scripture

PRAYER POINT:

Overcome Bad Habits, Strongholds, Addictions

INSPIRATIONAL QUOTE

"Feeling is the voice of the body; reasoning is the voice of the mind; conscience is the voice of the spirit."
~Kenneth Hagin

John 8:36

So if the Son sets you free, you will indeed be free.

Prayer

In the name of Jesus, I am free from every bad habit, stronghold, bondage, addiction, and generational curse. It is for freedom that Christ set me free. So I will stand firm in my freedom and not be entangled again with a yoke of bondage. Where the Spirit of the Lord is, there is liberty. The Spirit of the Lord dwells inside of me and I have absolute liberty from every work of darkness and every evil influence. Sin does not have dominion over me. In Jesus' name, Amen.

Weekly Devotions

YOU KEEP HIM IN PERFECT PEACE WHOSE MIND IS STAYED ON YOU, BECAUSE HE TRUSTS IN YOU. TRUST IN THE LORD FOREVER, FOR THE LORD GOD IS AN EVERLASTING ROCK. (ISAIAH 26:3-4)

Day Date Scripture

Special Notes

Day Date Scripture

Day Date Scripture

Day Date Scripture

Prayer List

Day Date Scripture

Day Date Scripture

Day Date Scripture

PRAYER POINT:

Inspirational Quote

"If we want to pour out God's love into the lives of our children, we must first receive it for ourselves."
- Joyce Meyer

Ephesians 2:10

For we are God's masterpiece. He has created us anew in Christ Jesus, so that we can do the good things He planned for us long ago.

Prayer

Father I dedicate these children to you. Let salvation and righteousness spring up within my children. May my children always be strong and courageous in their character and actions. May my children grow to find Your word more precious than gold. Help my children develop a strong self-esteem that is rooted in the realization that they are God's workmanship created in Christ Jesus. In Jesus' name, Amen.

Weekly Devotions

YOU KEEP HIM IN PERFECT PEACE WHOSE MIND IS STAYED ON YOU, BECAUSE HE TRUSTS IN YOU. TRUST IN THE LORD FOREVER, FOR THE LORD GOD IS AN EVERLASTING ROCK. (ISAIAH 26:3-4)

Day Date Scripture

Day Date Scripture

Day Date Scripture

Day Date Scripture

Day Date Scripture

Day Date Scripture

Day Date Scripture

Special Notes

Prayer List

PRAYER POINT:

Eating Surrounded By Enemies

INSPIRATIONAL QUOTE

"If God is going to feed you in the midst of your enemies, you have to be willing to sit at the table and eat surrounded by them."
~Teresa Wilson

Psalms 23:5

You prepare a feast for me
in the presence of my enemies.
You honor me by anointing my head with oil.
My cup overflows with blessings.

Prayer

Father, feed me in the midst of my enemies. Let me walk in the wisdom, knowledge and understanding that only comes from You. Deliver me from dream stealers and dream killers. Let me only look to You for divine direction. In Jesus' mighty name, Amen.

www.teresabwilson.com

Weekly Devotions

YOU KEEP HIM IN PERFECT PEACE WHOSE MIND IS STAYED ON YOU, BECAUSE HE TRUSTS IN YOU. TRUST IN THE LORD FOREVER, FOR THE LORD GOD IS AN EVERLASTING ROCK. (ISAIAH 26:3-4)

Day Date Scripture   Special Notes

Day Date Scripture

Day Date Scripture

Day Date Scripture   Prayer List

Day Date Scripture

Day Date Scripture

Day Date Scripture

Christine Spicer - Author: Christine lives in California and leads the "Power Up" prayer team. She is a prayer warrior, intercessor and has a passion to see people set free, healed & delivered. She enjoys praying for others & seeing God work right before her eyes. She is a wife to Charles and has 2 amazing boys, CJ & Justin.

Teresa B Wilson - Coach, Trainer & Speaker: Teresa is an ordained minister, author, speaker, entrepreneur and an expert in personal financial coaching. She is the founder of Abundant Life Group, Inc., a non-profit organization that helps struggling people around the world. Her life's passion is to help all of God's people who are struggling financially to live abundance. She travels the country teaching everyday people how to manage their faith and finances.

Lisa Lightfoot - Artist: Lisa is an artist from Wilmington, NC. She was awarded the "BEST IN ACRYLIC" category at the Landfall Foundation Art Show three years in a row. She has won many art awards over the years, and she says her success is nothing less than God's favor and it's all for His Glory.

www.ingramcontent.com/pod-product-compliance
Lightning Source LLC
Chambersburg PA
CBHW051454290426
44109CB00016B/1757